Body Maps

ELGA REÁTEGUI

Translated by

Álvaro Torres Calderón

Copyright © 2012 ELGA REÁTEGUI

All rights reserved. No part of this book may be reproduced in any manner without the express written consent of the Publisher, except in the case of brief excerpts in critical reviews or articles. All inquiries should be addressed to:

Pandora Lobo Estepario Productions, 1239 N. Greenview Ave. Chicago, IL 60642

All rights reserved.

ISBN: 1940856116
ISBN-13: 978-1-940856-11-7
Library of Congress control number: 9781940856117

To Álvaro Torres Calderón for the voices
and silences in the distance.

Contents

Wounds 5

Try it 6

Decision 8

Skin 9

Clairvoyance 10

Messages 11

The Date 12

No more 13

Wild Animal 14

A candle 16

Learning 17

The Way Back Home 18

Seed 19

Between Extremes 21

Antithesis 22

Experience 23

Speaking 24

Wood and fire	25
Painting	26
Light	27
I am	28
One Another	29
Equation	30
Viewpoints	31
On the road	32
Tide	34
Flashbacks	35
Fiction	37
Habits	38
You are my "ideal man"	40
Karma	43
Truth	45

PROLOGUE

Introduction from the translator

When I read this anthology of Elga Reategui's poems I was truly absorbed by the musicality and rhythm of the verses but also of the freshness and honesty of its content. It introspects in the individual world marked by the protagonists' experience. It shows different lives, voices that explore themselves for their own satisfaction and reflection. It is a shared experience facing the emotional and social pain. These worlds spin around a language full of balance and control, highlighting the human condition.

This is a book that moves smoothly and shows accurate images. Its language flows brilliantly and goes beyond the grammar of the senses. They provide hints of life, a revelation of being accompanied, a song to an eternal hope.

Body Maps, is a guidebook portraying different stages in life, in a woman's life: Moments of solace, moments of struggle, a constant reflection with oneself with an optimistic outcome. I honestly can say that the book moved me and revealed Reategui's mastery of describing feelings and images poetically, keeping consistency in the message of encouragement, living intensely, loving with all your heart, forgiving yourself and others, standing at the end of the day and saying "Yo soy" – I'm still here, I am what I am and that makes me authentic and human.

Finally, I would like to express my gratitude to Elga for her support about me translating her anthology, and my colleague Dr. Kristi Hislope for her encouragement and collaboration in revising the manuscript.

Álvaro Torres Calderón

BODY MAPS

Elga Reátegui Zumaeta   Translated by Alvaro Torres-Calderón

Wounds

The soul has deep holes
Wounds that won't heal
marks of incurable anomalies.

They are mixed in a
compendium of comforting proverbs,
in reflective therapy sessions;
in short romances that filled everything.
They have a season to bloom,
and another to disappear.
Timid and discreet
during their rest,
where they leave
mature flowers of joy;
they strengthen
castles of unbreakable
personality;
they feed indelible
love pacts
again.
Afterwards, the storm comes,
the unavoidable curse
of melancholy.
The wounds open up again,
the fluid leaks out again.

The soul has deep holes
Wounds that won't heal
marks of incurable anomalies

Elga Reátegui Zumaeta   Translated by Alvaro Torres-Calderón

Try it

If you'd like to explore
my rugged geography
you would find more than
three regions.
On my surface
I'm hurt
but in my core
you could find
something more valuable
than a treasure.

My elevated mountains
are warm
at their peaks,
a ray of your sun
would melt their daring cover
and you would see my fresh skin.

My deserts
are neither so quiet
nor sterile,
they carefully wait
a favorable season
to show off
their potentiality.

BODY MAPS

Perhaps drought
has aged my landscapes
prematurely;
perhaps downpour
has drilled holes in my face.
But hopefully waiting
for mild weather
could generously
give life to my
dying nature

Decision

If you'd like to come over
the night will last longer
freely, fully
and it would not feel like
leaving.

If you'd like to come over
the day will light up
widely, shinny
and it would never want
to go out.

If you'd like to come over
the noise would escape
boisterously, swiftly,
and you wouldn't have
a reason to complain.

Skin

Let me look under
your skin;
discover silently
your real essence
believe that a winged being
could exist
even when evidence
contradicts it.

Let me look under
your skin;
feel beforehand
the lukewarmness
of your foundation;
understand
that your human fickleness
can be forgiven
even when it kills a dream.

Let me look under
your skin ;
magically open
the gates of your
ethereal dimension;
knowing that in the deepest
we are a little God
although the other hurts a lot.

Clairvoyance

With eyes capable of seeing
at a distance
I will let myself
get to know you
today.

I will lift the sails
of a fine ship
to not be carried away
completely,
because I want
to be light.

I will set off
over the waves
of a waterless sea,
because I don't want
to get my wings wet.

With eyes capable of seeing
at a distance
I will recognize you
Again today.

Messages

I have to write
on water...
My thoughts with my fingers
on a wet board.
So no one
will see them
so no one will
understand them.

I have to draw
on the wind...
with my fingers
on a light wall
translate
my torment.
I will close my eyes
and cry inside
singing with your voice
in my temple.

Like water
like wind
return.

The Date

When they come to look for me
let me be alone.
With no more company
than myself
With an empty conscience
With a calm appearance.

When they come to look for me
let me be alone
with no more company
than myself
With my constant fears
With hidden sadness.

When I leave with them
Just let me go.

No more

You turned off the switch of life
like when
the candles of a Birthday cake
are blown out

An instant
a sigh
and no more.

In a snap of fingers
and life was shattered
it disappeared

You turned off the switch
and left us in the dark.

Wild Animal

Hunting a wild animal
unfriendly to formalities:
there is neither loyalty,
mutual belonging
nor fierce jealousy.

Standing firmly before the solace
of a wondering soul;
the voluptuousness
of an orphan tear longing for affection,
before timid kisses
on discover spaces to be stolen.

Hunting a wild animal...

On spontaneous vacation
the title holder hands over his post:
because of corporal boredom,
because of temporary freedom
or undefined sexuality.

Wild beast on occasion
eating the skin of abandonment.
Seasoning self-esteem
with igneous comments
of a pseudo protecting lover.

BODY MAPS

Empirical psychologist,
analgesic wizard;
there is no stability with you
nor individual control.
Crucial element
in your liberal chemistry.

Elga Reátegui Zumaeta   Translated by Alvaro Torres-Calderón

A candle

Light a candle
to brighten my gray sky:
transforming my depths
into a clear spring;
drinking my silence
from a crystal glass.

Light a candle
to brighten my gray sky:
Look at me in the reflections
of polished mirrors;
Kiss me on the petals
of my rising desires.
☐

Learning

I've never known
how to say: "I love you"
without looking
into the eyes,
without half a smile,
without drumming
my fingers on the table.

I always believed
in the right season
to give flowers,
to dedicate
songs
and to taste
feelings.

I've never doubted
the good fortune,
the simplicity
of my life
and your
sole
presence.

And you see
me already
recounting
damages,
blaming
fragility
and seeing you leaving.

Elga Reátegui Zumaeta Translated by Alvaro Torres-Calderón

The Way Back Home

Until birds
find their way back home
I will wait
next to
my window

Sewing my dreams
on a large
fabric
I will ease
my anxieties
while waiting.

Stitch after
stitch
I will combine
the threads
of absence
imagining
their aerobic
flights.

Until birds
find their way back home
I will stand
behind my window.

Seed

I am within you
a growing root,
extension of states;
removing
emotions,
removing
memories
and expelling
old guests.

I am within you
a flower in full bloom
preparing its
charm,
rejecting
known
scents
and searching for
original
poses
facing the sun.

I am within you
A ripening
fruit
shaping its body,
polishing its skin
preparing sublime
nectars
in its womb

that
you can drink
after you
give yourself to it.

I am within you …

☐

Between Extremes

I will exist
in the magnetic attraction of two bodies
that avoided finding each other;
in the trap of solitude
hanging
in the intense closeness
of a sensual touch

It's a dangerous combination
when disappointment falls like a heavy veil.
In my memories
I punish the values
I archived in my brain.

Vital math
Principles without cure
Strict laws
Severe dogmas
Rebellious masks

I will live in
the casual relationship
of an unowned night;
in the enjoyment
of bodies lent to
the feeling.

Body literature
Grammar of the senses
Whispering conjugations
Tactile essay
Skin tanned by shame.◻

Antithesis

Abandonment
wanders across her skin
in light sighs,
the enormous scream
of an open wound.
With deadly experience
the ambiguous sadness
absorbs her fluids
with cotton

And her innocence is presumed
although everyone saw her nude
before unknown desires
And her innocence is presumed
although she declared herself
owner of passionate addictions.
The cruel sight of a close rival
intimidates her fake bravery,
frightens her intimacy
forcing her to accept
that she is damaged goods.

And her innocence is presumed,
disarmed before the power
of manly flowers
And her innocence is presumed
visiting the temple of enjoyment
which for many isn't common.here.

Experience

I don't feel guilty
of having been like all women,
of having been human,
of having sensitive skin to desire,
of being a guest on another's lips.

In forced exile
I melted like ductile metal,
malleable to forge;
and I was shaped to their desire
in an experimental job.

They stirred the raging flames
with basic fuel of my passion.
They built solid bars
with the stubbornness of my love.

And despite
my painful journey,
I don't have any regrets
of having been like all women:
generous in constant forgiveness,
dreaming about the scent of tenderness
a woman in her highest being.

☐

Speaking

Speak
Speak to me

with the privacy of the night
with the softness of a scent
or the anxiety of the encounter

Look
Look at me

with the nostalgia of a lamppost,
the greenness of a clover
o the clairvoyance of a feeling

Feel
Feel me

In the shivers in the cold,
the tiredness after a challenge
or in the magic of a prayer.

☐

Wood and fire

We are wood and fire
on this field of skin,
of passionate flora,
and seasonal fruits;
creating rituals that satisfy
your sun.
With music of heartbeats
with shared dances

We are wood and fire
in the pleasant tactile battle,
with confusion of pieces
longing cohesion;
deciphering codes
in pieces of skin.
Without a pearly moon
Without a silent night

We are wood and fire
friction
flame
emotion
Between you and me:
just wood and fire

☐

Painting

Paint roses of illusion
over this transparent sea,
Outlining the possibility of a route
in each wave.

And when I contemplate
your mirror
the fantasy
recreates
our moments.

And when I caress
your blanket
the magic
interlaces our
thoughts.

Paint over the effervescence
of this sea
white lilies of passion,
sensing the possibility of destiny
in each wave.

☐

Light

There is light in your eyes
when tenderness
in the form of a tear
moistens your eyelids.

There is light in your eyes
when beauty
paints peaceful landscapes
on your pupils.

There is light in your eyes
when justice
rests gently
on your gaze.

There is light in your eyes
when I can recognize you
through them.

☐

I am

I am the one who ignites
the sand of your body,
the one who extinguishes
the whirlwind of your throat
and the one who
prays for you at dawn.

I am the one who sows
in the land plots
of your hands,
the one who waters
the terraces of your lips
and the one who thinks about you
when she cannot see you.

I am the one who rides up and down
your highlands,
the one who adds up and substracts
your passion
and the one who is born and dies
with your voice.

One Another

Two people:
seeing each other
and not looking at each other
(who found each other
and will never meet

While one person
offers and gives;
the other one over there
takes and demands.

Two people:
who hear each other
and don't listen to each other
(who were born
and will not recreate each other)

While one
waits and understands,
the other,
ignores and soon
will forget.

☐

Equation

Fake script
defiance
on burnt
paper.

Preparing
to modify
the equation
where factors
will alter
the product.

If only math
was useful
to organize
human habits as well.

No contradictions
no assumptions.
□

Viewpoints

I have seen a tree cry
the course of a river altered
the illusion of a woman darkened.

I have heard the Earth protest
the logs of a promise crackling
a choir of rain singing out of tune.

I have felt the indifference of the stone
trust at sowing time getting clouded
the art of lying growing stronger.

☐

Elga Reátegui Zumaeta Translated by Alvaro Torres-Calderón

On the road

Knock! Knock!...

minutes, seconds...
at your ego's door.
Please, light
the darkness
with a little match
made of words.

Call me for nothing
just for the pleasure
of dialing
a number.

Codes!
Money converted
In digits.
The answer
through the headphone!

Ring! ring!

Hours, days...
Cheer me up in turbulence.
The hopelessness when I'm not needed.

A sigh in place
of my name.

Life through
electrical impulses.

BODY MAPS

Bell didn't think
about science,
he established
communication.

Please, the invention
defending
my nourishment.
A phone call to revive me.

☐

Elga Reátegui Zumaeta   Translated by Alvaro Torres-Calderón

Tide

High tide
low tide

Unleashed near-sightedness
in confused eyes.

Rehearsed kisses
in eager mouths

High tide
low tide

Predicted travels
by clairvoyant minds
Guided habits
by astral patterns.

Made up fair
by mediocre
artists.

Fortune guide
Tributes to the moon.

☐

Flashbacks

Out of the scene
Dismiss
the main character

General protest
Changing history
because it didn't want
to play

Romantic disproportion
She = puro corazón
He = half-hearted enjoyment

Change the plot
Look for the replacement
bi-monthly romance
unilateral flirtation

I demand an explanation!

I'm not like everyone
I'm special

Don't complicate
yourself

Why
complicate
your life

New chapters
Surprise episodes

Elga Reátegui Zumaeta   Translated by Alvaro Torres-Calderón

Modified scripts
sudden distances

Rehash of thinking
about the future

rebel experiences
backward tongue twisters
☐

Fiction

Don't harm
Don't pull the petals off the flower
Don't cancel the desperate scream
Don't interrupt the sleepless night.

Don't harm
Don't stir up pain
Don't dry the wet patio
Don't light the day lamp.

Better:
Drink confidently
the humidity of my soul
Eat eagerly a thousand pieces
of an elusive heart.

But... don't harm.
☐

Elga Reátegui Zumaeta   Translated by Alvaro Torres-Calderón

Habits

A vote of trust
in the intimate stage
of a relationship.

I follow the game rules.

I warn you

I anticipate the possible
disobedience:
to my rigid codes,
in the absence of forgiveness,
in the break-up of trust.

Come:
bite the bone of
contention;
grab the hands
of distance;
feed the last
of my sensorial neurons.

A vote of trust
in the intimate stage
of a relationship.

So far I arrive,
I arrived, I will arrive...

I escape through the tiny eye
of time's

lock;
through the buttonhole
of your shirt's
first button;
through the gray ring
of the cigarette
that you tried
to put out.

A vote of trust;
with a prayer's
amen
to your divinity;
with the happy ending
of a story
that you didn't want
to live..
☐

You are my "ideal man"

You can cure my wounds
with tenderness...

The relaxing powers
of your caress in my hands;
the slow and silent touch
of your lips
on my shoulders;
The widespread passion on my skin
when you give yourself to me
are my best medicine
when emptiness attacks my world.

You in the sensuousness
of abandoning
reality
and throwing yourself
completely
to the madness of fusioning
worlds.

Where arbitrary time
disappears
and that space is nothing
when you love me.

Where my fears find
a refreshing rest
on your lips.

And it is because you can touch
perfection

BODY MAPS

when your eyes
shine clearly and reflect
the purity of colors.

And it is because you can be my ideal man
when you untie the ribbons
of your sensuality
and your manly instinct
can encourage my fantasies
of unity.

You can cure my wounds
with tenderness...

You can declare ownership
of the fertile areas of my body,
you can drink water from my fountains
and stir up my heart
with the violence of an explorer.

You are "my ideal man"
in the pleasure
of the skin,
the pleasure
of anxious mouths
and the perfect fit
when making love

You are "my man"
in the chess game
of ulterior motives;
the curiosity
of the attractive
enigma

and
the strength of the
sensorial game.

Indomitable souls
Temptations to be discovered
mysterious lands
hard to penetrate
and you don't let me love you.

But...
only you
can cure my wounds
with tenderness.

☐

Karma

Eternal return
the ebb and flow
of the sea
Many faces in one.

Rented body
karma transformations:
patching the soul
disguising the mind.

Apply the method
to adorn
your ordinary speech.

Satirize
Poison
Shake your
tablecloth
of emotions
run away from them
with the traumatic
ping pong of the escape.

Scream the impotence
to resort to abandonment
The glory of hiding
at work

Repress insanity
Not risking
good judgment.

Eternal return:
recycling bodies
reviving ghosts.

Truth

The truth is:
I don't trust you anymore
when I'm in your embrace
or when you swing me at your pleasure
but I still fall asleep (in your arms).

ABOUT THE AUTHOR

Elga Reátegui Zumaeta

(Writer and Journalist)

Born in Lima. Lives in Valencia (Spain). Studied Communication Sciences at the University Garcilaso de la Vega and graduated in Journalism at the University Jaime Meza Bausate at the Peruvian capital. Practiced in various media and delved into the world of literature with her book of poems Ventana Opuesta (1993), which was followed by Entre dos polos (1994), Alas de acero (2001), Etérea (2004), En mi piel (2005); also, with writer and decimista, Pedro Rivarola (now deceased) published the epistolary Correo de Locumba (2002) and Violación de correspondencia (2003), along with the poetry chapbook Madera y fuego and the CD Abrazados (2003).

In 2007 she published her first novel entitled El Santo Cura. Two years later, in 2009, it came to Peru in a second edition that was in charge of Editorial Group Arteidea.

Her book of poems En mi Piel is a compilation of her previous publications. The book contains illustrations by the talented artist Asun Perea Valencia Ferrer.

Elga has a blog that bears her name, where she conducts interviews with cultural, artistic and communications personalities, also a YouTube channel where cultural programs broadcast as Momentos (which she produces and leads), and an audio space area in which she has posted part of her poetic material.

In October 2012, she visited the United States revealing her literary production in several libraries and other cultural venues. In December 2012, she presented her second novel De ternura y sexo at the Guadalajara International Book Fair (Mexico).

The English version of her poems En mi Piel is this version under the title Body Maps.

She is a member of PEN Club International and the Association Concilyarte.

Her links are:
http://elgareategui.blogspot.com.es/
http://www.youtube.com/user/elgareategui/videos
http://loslibrosdeelgareategui.wordpress.com/
http://www.goear.com/Elga45/sounds

Elga Reátegui Zumaeta   Translated by Alvaro Torres-Calderón

ABOUT THE TRANSLATOR

Alvaro Torres-Calderón was born in Lima, Perú on April 18th, 1975. He received his degree in Law and Political Sciences at the Universidad de Lima. He went on to earn a M.A. degree in Romance Languages from The University of Memphis and a Doctorate in Spanish from Florida State University. His specialization is 19th and 20th Century Latin American Literature. He is Associate Professor of Spanish at the University of North Georgia. His publications include: "Alejo Carpentier y el Hombre Fronterizo: Una Constante en el Reino de Este Mundo" for the book Alejo Carpentier ante la crítica. Caracas, Monte Avila. 2005. He has contributed the article "Nación, Identidad y Frontera en la Prosa de Clorinda Matto de Turner" to the Peruvian Literary Journal Tinta Expresa His book of poems, Claroscuro, was published in Lima, Línea Andina. 2010. He also published several poems for the Stonepile Writers' Anthologies Volumes 1, 2 and 3 from the University Press of North Georgia. He was a guest writer for the Miami digital literary and art journal Sub-Urbano from August 2013 until February 2014, and contributed several poems or guest readings to the blogs Arcos de Reflejos, Con Tinta and The Cossack Review respectively. His interests include translations, music, film, theater, cuisine, integration law, Latin- American and Spanish female writers, José Martí, and Latin American civilization.

BODY MAPS

Elga Reátegui Zumaeta   Translated by Alvaro Torres-Calderón

PUBLISHER

Pandora lobo estepario Productions
http://www.loboestepario.com/press
Chicago

Cover photograph
Miguel López Lemus©

Model
Anastasia Arteyeva

www.ingramcontent.com/pod-product-compliance
Lightning Source LLC
Chambersburg PA
CBHW071759040426
42446CB00012B/2628